ANSWER TO BLUE

Other Books by Russell Thornton

The Fifth Window (2000)
A Tunisian Notebook (2002)
House Built of Rain (2003)
The Human Shore (2006)
Birds, Metals, Stones & Rain (2013)
The Hundred Lives (2014)
The Broken Face (2018)

Russell Thornton

Answer to Blue

HARBOUR PUBLISHING CO. LTD.
P.O. Box 219, Madeira Park, BC, VON 2H0
www.harbourpublishing.com

EDITED by Silas White
FRONT COVER ART Adobe Stock © Djero Adlibeshe
COVER AND TEXT DESIGN by Shed Simas/Onça Design
PRINTED AND BOUND in Canada
PRINTED ON 100 per cent recycled paper.

Harbour Publishing acknowledges the support of the Canada Council for the Arts,
the Government of Canada, and the Province of British Columbia through the
BC Arts Council.

LIBRARY AND ARCHIVES CANADA CATALOGUING IN PUBLICATION
Title: Answer to blue / Russell Thornton.
Names: Thornton, Russell, author.
Identifiers: Canadiana (print) 20210263938 | Canadiana (ebook) 20210263946 |
    ISBN 9781550179675 (softcover) | ISBN 9781550179682 (EPUB)
Subjects: LCGFT: Poetry.
Classification: LCC PS8589.H565 A82 2021 | DDC C811/.54—dc23

Contents

I

II

III

I

Blinds

Close them if you want. Or open them.
The set of blinds is the hostage of our eyes.
Turn the tilt wand with your exquisite fingers
and flip the slats as if signalling an SOS.
Close them if you want. Or open them.
You, me, you, me, you, me, you, me.
Whatever either of us sees is a lie.
Each of us is the hostage of the other.
Across the street through apartment windows,
people look out behind their own sets of blinds.
Our eyes are also the hostages of our eyes.
Our aluminum slats, factory cut and painted
the colour of puffy white clouds—
Close them if you want. Or open them.
We overlap and share blind desire.
Our set of blinds wants to detach itself
from its head rail and installation bracket,
its tilt wand and lift cord with it,
flapping wings and flying away
opening and closing on whatever is nowhere
and there, or nowhere and here;
to be more unknown to us than before,
fashioned for flight, flashing bright alarm.

Hinge

Before the door at the back of the eye.
—Matt Rader, *Visual Inspection*

A hinge, one part stationary,
fixed to a door frame,
one part swinging as a door swings,
and the middle part,
the hollow cylinder part.
Legs that let me walk
here and there,
hands that let me wave
hello and goodbye,
flesh that clasps and carries
the marrow while it flows
along the aisles
within the skeleton,
eyes that look. I am a hinge
when I speak, a hinge
when I say nothing. A hinge
when I frame a caress,
a hinge when I hold a weapon.
I recall saloon doors
opening inward, RCMP
striding in throwing people
to the floor. The hinges
were fastened to the law.
The rust of the hinges
that swung the rained-on doors
collected in foam-brimmed glasses
gathered on tabletops
like witnesses. I am a hinge

when my eye pupils widen,
a hinge when they contract.
A hinge when I am in love
and the hinge is a criminal
bereft and made to die
to save my eyes. I am a hinge
when dawn light slides
along my limbs,
a hinge when I panic. A hinge
when I am eye to eye
with the morning sun
delivering its sentence
not in words but in light
like a single blood cell.
A hinge when I wait again
for my release,
a hinge when a door
opens as if for the last time
bringing me to my own face.
Legs that let me walk
here and there,
hands that let me wave
hello and goodbye,
flesh that clasps and carries
the marrow while it flows
along the aisles
within the skeleton,
eyes that look. I am a hinge
whether the hollow
cylinder is filled or empty.
A hinge when the marrow
rolls clear of my hellos

and goodbyes and wakes me,
a hinge when the wedding
touch of all air swings me
before there is any door
that will open or close
at the back of the eye.

Love Letters

I

While we were writing love letters,
roads were being torn up
for the installation of new water mains.
While we made our plans to be together,
flies landed on the eyelids of drought victims
on continents neither of us had visited.

While we fastened seatbelts
in separate airplanes that would take us
from our opposite corners of the world
to the various locales where we could meet,
our most recent letters would always cross.
And while we slept in taxis
and in clattering train compartments
in bedding grey with wear
on the way to our wedding,
maids prepared our honeymoon hotel room,
replenishing bars of soap, puffing pillows.

While the justice of the peace
recited the words that married us,
a fly buzzed around her head,
circling the piled high, spray-stiff burgundy hair
that resembled the Colosseum in Rome.
The bureaucrats employed there
in the Palace of Weddings
went to and fro, exiting and entering
the ornate rotunda like actors on a stage.

II

While unheard-of intense summer heat
came on and came on in our home city,
and men worked at resurfacing cracked roads
in new layers of asphalt,
we saw we were aging, our faces altering,
and we had our old letters notarized
and had true copies made,
all for our future reference and proof
that you and I had written the letters.

While we made new plans
to go on a trip again to some faraway place,
the end that our letters began
drew nearer and nearer to us,
like a fly we could not manage to swat
and dispose of in a wastebasket.

While we repeated our itinerary
and verified and double-checked dates and details,
we used words such as *Yes* and *We will*.
And while we signed travel documents
and put them away for safekeeping
until the time of our departure
as if slipping folded sheets into an envelope
and sealing it with a kiss before we mailed it,
we confirmed the truth that our kisses carried
of what would be left when we were no longer there
to remember or forget letters, or kiss.

Unfinished

I sit in a suburban public library
surrounded by shelves of books hammering and fettering
within their bindings
the fortunes of time that will not be uttered
yet will not be kept silent either.
I look up at clean silver duct lines, a massive puzzle
with elbows and connectors,
a system for guiding air.

My father's father, whose company
fabricated and installed
aluminum ventilation and heat ducts
concealed above suspended ceilings
in commercial buildings throughout the city
before the advent of industrial chic,
would, I imagine, have pronounced
the interior here unfinished.

My grandfather is finished. Likewise
my father who as a young man
laboured in his father's factories
and left his architectural metal art
of interconnected different-hued, different-shaped
pieces of steel to fall apart
at obscure locations.

The criss-crossing ducts hanging above me,
the rough unpainted concrete—
it is all as it is meant to be,
even if looking with this or with that eye
might lead me to believe otherwise.

Those two men measure, machine-cut, fuse conduit,
they leave me exposed
while I try to finalize myself,
redo again and again, carry out work
to execute what I think to be true of myself
and fulfill my own prophecy of release
which says what is unfinished
of them will be finished in me.

The Show Must Go On

The show must go on.
You tell me about touring Uzbekistan,
restricted to hotel rooms, given little to eat;
performing in women's prisons in Russia,
stage makeup hiding exhaustion.
I imagine you among the cast,
statuesque, Black Sea cheekbones,
glowing grey-blue eyes.
You stand with your back straight.
You give and give of your talent.

I have read how the lead in a British troupe
continued to perform *King Lear*
with air raid sirens accompanying
the old man's ravings, ceiling plaster
and dust plummeting around him
as bombs fell in World War II London.

And how a Hollywood actor
in a scene where his character
learns he has been tricked,
slammed his fist on a table,
breaking a glass and cutting his hand.
It was not part of the script,
but the actor did not break character;
the take was used with his real blood.

I keep in my memory a poet
recalling his middle years as "having
a nervous breakdown and not knowing it"—
when he was producing lyrics of praise,
doing what he needed to do to dominate
reality, offering up his masterpiece,
performing a jig before the holy nothing
within the chaos. The show must go on.

You play your various parts; I play mine.
You turn your face in this direction, that;
I do the same. And you are no longer you,
you are no one and I am no longer myself,
I am no one. We are like identical twins—
separated, raised apart, now desperate to meet.

We are here as suddenly as anything is;
we behold in us the nothing
that has brought us here
when we come to hold one another.
The nothing is as soon lost to us;
we are all we have as the way to remember.
Any story we create, any tale
we tell of ourselves—only ever able
to say goodbye—we cling to it here
where we have been abandoned to love.

Dumpster

Everything is marrying everything again.
You can smell it—
the waste overflowing the dumpster.
The thrown bouquet,
the glittering eyes, the grins,
the lucky couple,
the guests posing for photos—
it all comes back
in the plastic garbage bags heavy with slop.
Here in the dark
within a large metal box
the wedding vows are being taken again
in chemical utterances,
the *I do*s purer here
than in any other ceremony.
Now the men come with carts,
prop open the lid
and begin their search
for cans and bottles.
It may happen that scraps
of a tiered cake turn up.
Seagulls and crows
whirl around
the men's heads like angels.
They flap and hop
around the men's feet
as they come down the lane
crying divorce
from dumpster to dumpster.
But everything is marrying again,
couple upon couple
are marrying again

within the rot,
and the men who live on the rot,
who pick through
the wedding waste,
and cash in the refundables
to get high,
are marrying everything
again and again
within themselves.
When the truck
wide as the lane arrives
and a driver works controls
to lift and empty this dumpster,
the men scatter
like seagulls and crows,
take off pushing their carts
rattling like skeletons,
hurry away with their loot like time.

Breaking into the House of My Father's Father

There is no one home; I find an unlocked window,
open it and go through. I know I might hear a key edge
push pins, a cylinder slide a bolt and a door handle turn,
and I will be caught. It comes to me that he is dead
and has been for decades. Other people live here now.
My ears, my eyes may have had a place here once;
even so, the act I commit in this dream is forbidden.
He built this house. He lived here with his wife
and only child. Now they are all gone; I am aware of it.
Still I am afraid he will walk in and see me as an intruder.
I lie down in a bed somewhere within the house.
By sleeping I will do what I need to do. I understand
I am here to plant a hidden device that will allow me
to hear and see him in his basement workshop.
With lathe and miller and drill press and tools, he will
bring forth intricate machines. I prop my head
against the other side of the wall, and in my sleep
conduct surveillance. What he makes, concentrating force
and precise rhythm, begins to move. My senses
are no longer mine, they are powerful and subtle,
they detect his presence though he is dead.
A deep grandfather occupying the house brushes
against me. I feel the haunches flex then the pause
as the animal prepares to attack. When it springs
the darkness shifts, and becomes all of space.
I cannot tell whether I am prey or hunter,
the death in the sleep I have entered is change beyond
change, and I am older than my father,
who is present in a far corner of the house, a boy alone,
and older than my grandfather—I have gone past them,
and I kill and am killed and am born over and over
and over in this house in this sleep in this joy.

Travel Trunk

Here is the travel trunk that once carried the belongings of my father's mother. It is a large steamer trunk from the 1920s, brown canvas with wooden bandings, my grandmother's name stencilled in white at both ends.

The present occupant of the home that my grandfather built after World War II came across the trunk in a storage area of the house, contacted me and passed the antique on to me.

I can see my grandfather proposing to his bride-to-be to get into this trunk. And her getting in, smiling mildly, and lying down. And him sealing her in, snapping the brass latches shut, turning the skeleton key in the brass lock.

It must have been while they were on a steamer heading across the Atlantic for Canada that he sawed her in half.

I can see him spread wide the halves of the travel trunk, wave his hand through the space between, and confident because he is a man who is going places, fit the halves back together, drape a satin cloth over the trunk and utter words to go with his performance.

Then he whips away the cloth, undoes the latches, turns the key again and opens the case expecting to see her there in one piece, smiling.

But she is not there. Somewhere between their departure and their arrival, she has disappeared.

And I can see now that he made use of the empty trunk. I go through it and discover that he filled it with his papers—technical school diplomas, driver's licences, many sets of rolled blueprints, mostly of various vehicles he designed and built.

Maybe some descendant of some relation of hers who lives a continent or two away knows more of her than I do. I remember only a woman with a soft voice and an accent. Maybe they have done research, investigated her history, which my grandfather stamped with his name, and like me found only the idea of an old magic trick gone wrong, found they were an audience for time itself, and were left with nothing.

Anchor

Like a container ship being loaded to capacity,
a new house frame goes up two-by-four by two-by-four

on the site where we separated—my father;
me and one brother; my mother and two other brothers.

Our house did not pull up anchor,
it stayed there decades without us. When it was demolished,

and a truck came, and a massive bin, I was elsewhere—
I had entered my life as if sailing away.

And the anchors of ships now waiting in a line
in the inlet can be identified, each one

by the casting letters and numerals they were assigned
in the foundries where they were forged. The front door

of a new house has on it the numbers I carry in my head—
but the house is unfamiliar to me. The ships

display their names in house-high letters on their hulls,
but the languages are unknown to me.

And the more I look out to the strait and the horizon of cloud,
the more my eyes fail me like a small boat

driven back by wind to what I thought I had forgotten—
an unfinished basement, a room, a bed, a desk. Now I close my eyes

to see these things that stay exactly as they were
the hour they were suddenly gone; they are an anchor

though the anchor is weightless and its markings
match no official record of any ship or harbour.

Design

External life being so mighty, the instruments so huge and terrible, the performances so great, the thoughts so great and threatening, you produce a someone who can exist before it. You invent a man who can stand before the terrible appearances ...
  —Saul Bellow, *The Adventures of Augie March*

With excavators and bulldozers
they are torturing the creek banks,
with asphalt laying new thoroughfares,
with loops of traffic tightening their hold
on the waters swerving and descending
to the level run to the creek mouth.

What do you see? my father asked me
the evening of the day I found him
after years of looking for him—
he turned to me, magnificently high,
as he drove me around in his car.

I see disaster, he said, waving his finger
with great panache at passing buildings—
architect-cum-artist-cum-drug dealer,
he would redesign it all.

I remember I stood and proudly told
everyone in my grade one class
how he parked his car in front of our house
facing the wrong way on purpose;
the tickets piled up on the mantel.
(Decades later, the street is a one-way
to regulate the commuter flow.)

I remember I spent an afternoon
with him when I was a child—
I brought along my dog
(later taken away for frightening people);
I waded into these pale-green waters
to grab some caught, glinting object
and the current pulled me down,
but I reached and righted myself to a bark.

Now I would redesign myself
under the pounding bridge traffic
like the ripples in the creek water
redesign themselves as they pass
between and over the creek rocks
strewn down the bed of glacial till—

like the ripples I watch arrive and vanish
and arrive again before the terrible
appearances of the highway interchange
and cars and trucked-in gravel.

I would redesign myself and stand
in the architecture of myself
even as I give myself up—
in the father ripples, the son ripples,
while the waters flow straight into the sea.

Tiger's Paw

I

The trapped wind swerves; the branches of the creek-bank trees bend and begin to break; the creek waters beat; the rocks leave their outlines; what is lunging there takes on talons of rain and slashes the air.

II

A man walks along a street hearing his own mind shackling itself; he is a narrow entryway—and lying in wait, in relentless awe, in ecstatic rage, in radiant need, he undoes the ratio of himself, unlocks the error. Somewhere he will offer a wandering, cursed woman a gentle touch.

III

There is a pool in the creek, a killing eye—a lid now closed over it, a spell. There is a cat settling into the lap of the glacial till at the hearth of the ravine and falling asleep.

IV

Furious water will lift into street-side flower petals, circle up into a blueness. Open to the slightest wind, this flower will lift, a child suddenly wrinkling, a murderer weeping, a hand.

V

The tiger has been here a long, long time. The rain will thicken and sweep; the creek will surge and grow wild; the ravine will be a transparent screen— with a paw tearing its way through it.

The Prometheus Eye

I taught them modes of prophecy ... I showed them the mottled beauty of the
well-formed liver ... I cleared their sight for the signs within flames.
    —Aeschylus, *Prometheus Bound*

                        ... every thing has its
Own Vortex ... he perceives it roll backward behind
His path, into a Globe itself enfolding, like a sun ...
    —William Blake, *Milton*

When a crow swerves towards me blocking out the sun,
the crow and the black pupil find one another.

The birds riding the air the length of continents—
they drop out of the sky; they discover their feeding places gone.

Teens thieve love in alleyways, see police arrive—
headlights blind them; officers shine flashlights into their smiles.

How is it that a story renders me—
makes me what I am that I say of a thing, "It is beautiful"?

When a crow flaps up, lands on a dumpster
and jumps to slash and feast on mangled, blackened meat,

the pupil disappears—and grows back again,
displaying pictures of arrested light to the sun.

When the crow swerves down again cawing and wanting to eat,
the pupil ventures, consumes itself—

lit narrow and beholding many, lit wide and beholding one.
In its story it is marrying every living, dying thing,

delivering itself to prophetic colour, cutting a path,
giving the faraway fire of the sun its eyes here in the dark.

Murder Book

Here it is, a ring-shaped plot
off some remote highway exit.
You dream it, you draw it
in your murder book
like a detective who discovers it
after years of tracking a suspect.
All around you, the victims
buried in concentric circles.
He has created this site
in dry earth on open land.
It is where he held
their faces and soothed them asleep.
He killed them the way he slit
the throats of deer, or swiped
two fingers along a small screen.
You stand at the centre
of this immense zero
and know this is the end
of your murder book.
Your sketches, your notes
will only lead you
back to a blankness
like the one you imagine he saw
in the children's eyes
before he erased those eyes.
You know he has vanished
and you will find no clue
to whom he might be.
What is left for you
is to witness each of the children
be carefully dug up,
identified and returned home,

and to file your murder book,
and believe a God exists who sees
briefly in every newborn's face
his own face for the first time
before he turns to the beauty
of another and another,
but must turn now to conduct
his own search for the route that brought
the murderer to this place,
and that is why he has gone out
on the roads and cannot be found.

The Notes That Are Left

The cruellest notes, the sweetest.
The notes behind the lilting solo.
The notes of the black light
of the animal in swerving desire.
The notes among the emaciated
out on the roads
among heaped corpses.
The notes that tend the diseased,
that move through semen,
that circle through wind-scoured skulls,
that swell within the egg.
The notes of the birth canal.
The notes that remain
when all else has been exhausted.
The notes that embrace ghosts,
that sit with lover and beloved
beneath blossoming apple trees.
The notes of the small boy
fleeing his country
with his family
to lie face down dead
on an island beach.
The notes that tell the story
of all the other notes.
The notes of peace,
of the bride of quietness,
of a holy mother and child.
The notes that are blacked out
naked nipples and vaginas
in a magazine.
The notes that are love
stronger than death.

The notes that are not there and there
like a letter in the name of G-d.
The notes that are smashed windows
and burned down houses,
that are the fragments
of destroyed temples—
walls of great blocks of stone
and openings between them
that travel forever.
The notes so remote
in their loneliness
that when they are played
you can barely imagine the instrument
or the fingers plucking strings
as anything but breath.
The notes that are whisperings
from the centre of the song,
that float around the melody.
The notes that are left
when all the other notes
have been played
yet can never be altered
without altering the song.
The notes that arrive
out of the deepest listening
as if always for the first time.
The notes that are still
only the lost echoes
of the notes
in every true song.

A Sign

Not a fastened-on letter of the words *City Hall*
will remain when almost every structure here is suddenly gone.
And of the mayor and councillors, and the chambers
where debate is held on bylaws and resolutions,
and decisions are made as to the things that will be removed,
and the things that will go in their places—maybe nothing will remain.

And maybe nothing of the two of us—
and the independent government we thought we created,
and the infinite agreement we felt we arrived at,
and even the perfect law we imagined we enacted when,
entwined, we wrote out our own and each other's names
in what we called the language of air and light and rain and earth.

And maybe nothing of any standing tree—growth ring
upon growth ring now a single, immense, unseeable zero;
branches of side-by-side trees lifting their new leaves together
to share clear sunlight now a lost memory.
Maybe only a large, rectangular, thick metal sheet
undestroyed, still upright—only the now-blank weathering steel

that was put up outside a building entrance
to take clean, sweeping rain in its chemical arms,
and after a few seasons make a patina
that would endure and roughen and become grainy,
and turn the colour of living cedar bark—
maybe only this will survive the blast of unnatural weather.

Now if people are alive, they will be gratefully blind
in the way that their eyes will have forgotten them,
and the self-layering, deepening reddish-brown of the rust
will be for them a sign of secret meetings being held below ground,
wordless unions within hidden water, sightless root systems
at work restrengthening intimacies, remaking trees.

II

II.

Story of Mist

Morning mist is caught in mountainside trees
like the horns of a male sheep in a dark thicket.

The mist will burn off with the day,
be offered up like the animal laid on piled wood in place of a son.

Here I am, calls out all there is to see,
and the light of the eye makes a sacrifice

of itself to become human sight. The ram seems to weep,
and the mist clasps the tree branches

even as it melts and runs down the air.
Every wondering, wide question my small son asks me

makes me bleat within, and makes the mist
that I am disappear. I see him alone

on the altar of time. I do what time tells me, I grab at faith
that he will remember I love him.

Coyote

Clear, pale blue, electric flash at the edge of sight—
a set of eyes arrived out of a block of woods
to jerk my hands from the steering wheel. I ran the vehicle

half onto the curb. I was driving I had no idea where
after dropping off my daughter at kindergarten;
there it was on the sidewalk, wolf-like but smaller, slenderer,

large ears, slim, pointed muzzle, diseased-looking, alerted—
now the only real thing in the blinding morning.
I had watched as my daughter danced away—

Little girl, I heard myself say, print perfectly,
excel at numeracy, thrill to your turn as special helper,
listen to a story with all you are, be rapt before a chrysalis.

I have come to a dark barrier beyond which I cannot go—
I have brought it here and met it here; I cannot see into it
and I beg it to break and open within me

and let me know it as its friend. In a picture book, remember,
I read to you a timeless story about a coyote
that accompanied the first man and woman

into the physical world. At recess, run out
to the meeting place where you tell jokes in a circle of children;
run out into the arms of the sunlight in the school field—

the ecstatic daughter of the original couple
now lost to one another. Now learn the planets' names
and do your sharing in class on a creature of the wild

while I circle my own words not baring my teeth. Draw, paint.
Make collages, mosaics. At noon, sit with your fairy lunch kit
and friends Vidia, Luna, Silvermist, Iridessa and Tink.

At three o'clock, I will come to the edge of the playground
to wait for the quick touch of your small hand—
as if I have driven away never to come back, and yet come back;

what is laughter in you and leaves your lips freely
is in me a howl I keep at the bottom of my throat
out of fear it will become sound and I will lose you in the light.

Shore

The events of childhood do not pass but repeat themselves like seasons of the year.
        —Eleanor Farjeon

When she told me an infestation had ruined the yard
and it had taken a year to clear it away
and get the lawn going again,
I thought I heard her refer to the Silver Beetles.

We had wandered far on bicycles,
my small son and daughter and I—
to the rise of a block with a swerving view
of forested mountains on one side,
yellow and black mountains of sulphur and coal
down near the water on the other,
grain elevators, hundred-car-long freight trains,
and farther out, a bridge vaulting an inlet,
and in the sky a sun like an immense guitar.

When we came to where she stood
tending shrubbery and early summer flowers,
I thought for a moment I knew her—
she was the lady with short, rough, corn-coloured hair
who worked at the store around the corner
and who made up perfect bags of ten cents'
worth of candy for kids, and seemed lonely.

But no, that lady had been old even then—
and when I told the woman I spoke with now
that I had lived on this block as a child,
she told me she had resided here in this house
for a great many years, but that I may have known
the previous owners, whose name had been Shore.

Yes, their name had been Shore—I remembered—
and the sound of the name was a plucked note
that reverberated through me and I ran again
from my old house in the middle of the night
out along the block up the hill of a dark wave
to a covered porch where a woman opened a door
and brought me to the safe shore of her home.

And when I showed my two children the house
where I had lived when I was around their ages,
or rather the house that had been built in its place,
I heard myself read out loud the three numbers
on the front door—I remembered the numbers—
and count out for myself and my children
an odd time signature the same way
I had tried to teach myself and my three brothers
vocal harmonies in the pretend cover versions
of the British Invasion hits we performed
in sets of pajamas on our stage of cement basement floor.

And while we rode away along the sidewalk,
the green within the green of the grass
all down the block still held a silver it would keep
as it swept into the blades, the cared-for trees
still held leaves that were fresh notes
they would lift together as they accomplished their melodies,
and whatever I remembered or did not remember,
I let my children take from me without their knowing
as they pedalled ahead of me, the two of them
returning me to the quick drum intro and rhythm strum,
the melodic bass line, the pithy licks and solo
of a song I used to sing again and again.

The Blue Boy

In front of my kids' school
a miniature squall lessens as if on cue
and mist moves in from a forest offstage—
an enormous neon replica
of Thomas Gainsborough's life-sized portrait
of a boy outfitted in shining blue.

My grandmother is hitting her marks
on the floor of the world again
and reciting just beyond hearing a speech
in which she orders her morning coffee
at a counter in the Blue Boy Hotel—
a building named for the painting
and blue-trimmed inside and out—
before she heads across the street
to the day job she has done for forty years.

This is when I know to step out to the mist
from under heavy tree branches—
and the rain increases, and its curtains close
as glittering theatre curtains close;
the rain increases again—
the curtains open again.

I see my kindergartener walk out
of the school doors with his classmates;
almost immediately he lowers his eyes.
To keep the rain from his face?
To keep me from seeing
as he glances towards our place?
He could be bowing his head in prayer.

I stand and wait as if I have always waited
exactly here for exactly these events to occur—
for blue mist and my grandmother to arrive
between what changes and does not change;
for rain to increase once again
as if on cue as the mist vanishes, a spirit
losing its hold on the brightened air.

And for the work of her visit to be complete:
to remind me the way she can
that my five-year-old will be looking for me;
to tell me I must stand solid and visible
so he cannot fail to see me.

I nod to him now; he feels it is okay to nod back.
No two as unmistakable to each other—
me in my soaked shirt; him in his blue nylon jacket
and looking out from the portrait
the calm rain makes of him,
my blue boy in the rain.

Debt

Surprise cold. Great plummeting snowfall.
Thank God my kids have snow boots, proper coats.
The year my mother
sweet-talked a salesman
into giving her a department store charge card
(Eaton's? Sears?)
suddenly we all had winter clothing.

A month or so later, the twice-a-day
phone calls and daily raps on the door.
My mother hid; I answered,
stood there scared, ashamed,
and made up endless stories to keep fates at bay.
She had no intention
of trying to make the payments.

Never warmer outside
in any winter ever again, my younger brothers and I—
except one of us
who could never get warm.
Flapping-soled runners and socks on the hands,
or boots and actual mitts,
it didn't matter, he was always freezing.

Forty years later, he finds out
he has a medical condition
that makes him feel the cold more than other people.
And me, I'm building snow forts
for my two small kids
to crawl into and sit as in a cozy home
in their expensive snowsuits.

The sun that arrives
to sit low in the sky wrapped in a white cowl
rises through my boy and girl
rising where it begins
and makes the snow world bright.
I tell myself I'll never have to borrow
to keep my kids protected from anything including cold.

But the cold that my brother
could never escape, his body making him pay
as the temperature went down,
was him always knowing better,
and every degree below zero that we are warm now
is a creditor I must face at the door of the present
and lie to regarding my whereabouts.

Smitty's Burgers

Five bucks bought us
four plain Smitty's burgers (75 cents each),
four pops (25 cents each) and four bags of chips (25 cents each).
So cheap that it was hard to believe even back then.
Who knows what was in the patties.
We grew up on rubbish.
My own kids—when I try now
to introduce them to anything
non-organic, non-Whole-Foods
just for the retro fun of it, look at me like I'm nuts.
But I'd be happy
to fill them up with rubbish on a regular basis
if I could give them one dinnertime
like the ones my three brothers and I had with my mom
when she came home and handed us money and told us
to go down the street to Smitty's and get our dinners.
Kids we met at school
had dinner at the same hour every evening
and had to wash their hands and had manners
and ate roast beef and potatoes and vegetables
and home-baked desserts,
and had after-dinner homework and rules,
all presided over by moms and dads
at opposite ends of dining room tables.
We had a welfare witch mom
who, just like that, let us buy dinner.
We knew what people said about her—
she was young enough
to be our older sister ... and where was the husband?
We saw them look away from her.
We knew it and were ashamed.
But we also weren't.

When she gave us the word and we went off to get dinner,
we ran as fast and as effortlessly as people do in dreams,
and we ran all the way there and back in the dazzle
of our mother's green eyes and when we sat down
and unwrapped our dinners, it was hard to believe,
but we dined together like princes on Smitty's burgers.

Floaters

When I try to look at them, they dart away.
They move as my eyes move, they drift, debris
underwater, when my eyes stop moving.
When I look at white paper, there they are;
when I look at clear sky, there they are—
black strands I cannot get out of my eyes.
They swing in the corners of my eyes
like hanging rope swinging in the gallows.

Fibres, they are microscopic fibres
within the chamber of the vitreous humour.
They have clumped and pulled away from the retina,
and are casting shadows on the retina. My eyes
themselves spin the fibres and interlace the strands.
The sharp flashes I see at my periphery—
the retina severing; I wait for the displays
to trick me with light at the denouement of sight.

My eyes' pupils like any eyes' pupils
have used sunlight as thread and weaved rainbows.
Like any eyes' pupils they will weave webs,
each knot tying a jewel of every datum,
each jewel tied to every other jewel,
each jewel reflecting every other jewel—
within black circular openings they will weave
their webs of appearances to catch fates like prey.

The eye will play Athena, the eye will play Arachne—
Athena depicting the immortals' glories;
Arachne portraying Zeus's offenses—as a swan
he rapes Leda, as a satyr he entices Antiope.
Athena will destroy the mortal woman's loom
and tapestries. Arachne will prepare a rope of thread
to hang herself; Athena will change the noose
into a cobweb and Arachne into a spider.

The eye will hunt its story as if a story is a fly—
draw it to where it sits at the centre of its web,
at the hub of its wheel, where it will unravel the fly.
The eye will hunt light for its sight, will drop
darkness like a hood over a head to hang the light—
and my eyes do this now; they break and dangle
from their transparent tissue by their dark threads,
they witness their own floating in the floating world.

Exit

There are always EXIT signs everywhere.
Sometimes the lights inside the signs are out,
like failed torches in a network of mountain signal fires.
Sometimes an arrow appears after the word EXIT
pointing a direction out—this way, that way.
And every arrow points to another arrow.
Kani krio exo, a Greek woman declared to me.
I laughed because it was the beginning of summer.
Yes, it's cold out, I said, this way, that way.

That woman would become old and die in her bed
where she had spent the nights alone her entire life
except for a single week in a hotel suite
as a newlywed on a springtime honeymoon.
When she and her husband arrived back home
and the man's mistress was waiting at the train station,
the woman immediately exited her marriage.
It happened she was already pregnant with a daughter
whom I would fall in love with two decades later.

There are always EXIT signs everywhere.
And in one of the occupations I find myself in now
I keep an array of EXIT signs in good repair.
I set up ladders, I climb to remove plate covers
and I replace bulbs to ensure signs stay lit brilliant red
to comply with city fire safety regulations,
using bulbs guaranteed ten thousand hours of life,
more time than the year we split, reunited, split,
argued trying to find a way to stay together.

And every EXIT sign leads to another EXIT sign—
and there will always be lights I need to replace,
until I suddenly go out myself and am gone.
In the building I take care of, if there is a loss of power
the emergency batteries will run the EXIT signs
even when all the other lights have died,
but it won't matter, there will be nowhere to go,
none of the EXIT signs will be necessary,
the inside will be the dark outside, the outside the inside.

Looking Good

Looking good, I wrote to her
when she emailed me a photo, but I didn't mean it.
Black hair newly blonde, new face,
newly engaged, she was feeling good—
and I pretended and said what I said.

We were together when we were young,
and then not together, and I never saw
the lines that were surgically swept away.

I imagined that I began tracing the face
I had touched two, three decades before—
before it became middle-aged,
and before the skin was then cut and refitted.

My fingers followed quickly where I thought
time must have made its way gradually
around her eyes and mouth and neck.
I wanted to touch where the loosening skin
and subtle hollows and shadows first appeared,
and find I was that close to her again,
and where I had often been untruthful
I now wanted to say only exactly what I meant.

But my fingers lost the way—the face
was neither the face I did not touch as she aged,
nor the face of the twenty-year-old I did touch.

And whatever the chances that time
could have continued to touch time and praise it
through the two of us, or that lines and wrinkles
could have made themselves vanish, the chances were gone—
along with my being able to say to her
that she was looking good, that she was looking
more than good always, and not be lying.

A Cup of Coffee

We forgot we had coffee in front of us
and after a while it sat there untouched
as if our hours of talking had forced it
to be partially drunk the same in both cups,
the way the law of gravity makes any liquid find its level.

We forgot and did not care where we were
when we nestled in a dark far corner
of a rundown restaurant named Lentzos—
where they never bothered us, never kicked us out,
but instead gave us a place to stay all night.

When a long time later I looked for you,
I found only addresses in different cities
and phone numbers no longer attached to you,
finally only dates after "born" and "deceased."

Now, later still, I briefly visit where I once lived,
and look for Lentzos—Montreal landmark
at the corner of Guy and St. Catherine—
and see it gone and new buildings everywhere.

And I arrive at another café and order a coffee.
I sip until it finds its level as if the cup
sits on the table in a back booth at Lentzos
and still holds my future within it—though it will
never be turned upside down then right side up
and the images and shapes read in the grounds.

If I let half the coffee stay and go cold,
it will be because I have looked for you
through pictures that show themselves in my memory
knowing you are there but unable to see you clearly,
and I want to keep even what I cannot remember.

If I drink the coffee, all of it, like a potion,
it will be because I want to fall away
to where my memory finds its level apart from me,
as if I am lost within what I cannot see
and have no need to remember what I cannot leave,
and the coffee I taste is all the coffee
I did not drink with you when you were alive.

The Other Life

I

Before it is light, the small birds will begin to chirp together. In an hour I will wait for the clock radio to display six o'clock and blare news, and I will know again I will die soon enough—and elsewhere I will have been murmuring into dense, dark air, *I was young, I was this, I was that, I'm sorry, I wish.*

II

A disc in my lower back has shifted and ruptured, and the material leaking out of its rubbery sac is meeting nerve tissue for the first time. If I try to move, I will hear the nerves' response along my spinal canal. And elsewhere the repair that began long before my back went awry will continue. All night in the dark on the precipice of a pillow and my resting forearm, I will undergo repair while you wander alone.

III

I will wake beneath a brightening window. And elsewhere a single bird will have dropped out of the sun to claw at and devour the dark. Where I have murmured and sung and my insides re-formed, the light will remove distances and years—and where I roll carefully out of bed I will trick the pain in my spine with medication; and later I will lie in the glare of an operating room far from where I murmured my way to endless repair and where I could hear you pleading in the dark.

IV

The chirping of the small birds will fade into the six o'clock news and early traffic noise. And elsewhere you will be wandering far and farther, worn down and frenzied and wanting to be scorched with flame or buried in earth or drowned.

V

Elsewhere, I will plead as you plead. The aloofness I showed will have brought me to where I am shackled to stone. And in a hospital room I will need the day as I need all the days allotted to me; they open the way to you. My lower spine will heal, and I will jump out of bed as I am programmed to do and walk upright free of pain, and I will leave you behind again and again. And I will not want the pretence or disguise. Even here in the day my back will never be as it was before it was operated on, the slipped world will never be as it was before; the news and the music issuing from the clock radio will never tell me of you.

VI

Elsewhere, my insides will re-form again, be torn from me again, and re-form yet again, and the wound will widen in the repair. The dark will be a dark beyond what I know in any outer night. If it is a memory, it is written in your body. If it is a prophecy, it is written in your body. And I will want to follow where you go finally to a river mouth, where the river's outflow lays its silt. That is when the bird that flies out of the sun will nest in the wound it made. And tend and sleep in the wound it made. And in the daylight, I will be true to a dark where I can be freed to be lost like you. The more I am nothing, the closer I come to you who have become nothing; the closer I come to a touch that restores whoever brings it into the day.

When I Do Not Love Her

... and when I love thee not/Chaos is come again.
—William Shakespeare, *Othello*

When I do not love her,
all the elements jumble together
in a shapeless heap
like our ravelled bedsheets.

When I do not love her,
we are two neighbouring
molecules of water
that have ended up
in different oceans.

When I do not love her,
all the birds around me
are in a race to nowhere.

When I do not love her,
I conclude that the chaos
of my feelings
is the true foundation of reality.

When I do not love her,
the value of our stock falls
and we sell
and make the stock fall further.

When I do not love her,
the intricate chaotic system
that synchronizes
the workings
of the cells of my heart
through my attraction to her
falls into an error of order
and my heartbeat loses its rhythm.

When I do not love her,
chaos reveals
its inner workings
and it is a clockwork of hate.

When I do not love her,
the predictability horizon
of love is the instant
of a look, a touch.

When I do not love her,
a butterfly flaps its wings
and causes a hurricane
half a world away.

When I do not love her,
we repeat ourselves
in a never-ending feedback loop
and I conclude again and again
that I never loved her.

When I do not love her,
as far as the laws of mathematics
refer to love,
they are not certain,
and as far as they are certain,
they do not refer to love.

When I do not love her,
chaos explores me
like a metaphor
for my not loving her
and for my loving her.

Two Poems about Dreams and Rain

I

We leave each other. Years later I happen to open a book
that I have left unread on a high shelf
and there I am, it seems, the main character sitting at a café window

watching cars going down a street,
headlights illuminating a long way through rain and darkness
and through innumerable flying drops to more rain and darkness.

There I am in the flashback with someone I have almost forgotten—
we are embracing in a tram in a foreign city
as if we are both going to die that minute.

II

We leave each other. I have a recurring dream I cannot recall,
though I feel I am different because of it—
I wake living a denouement I do not understand.

It is like when I have missed rain and run out
into the downpour in a faraway locale where it hardly ever rains,
and run out the same in my home city where it rains and rains.

It is like thinking I hear a seagull cry a thousand miles inland,
or a freighter blow a foghorn on a prairie highway,
or a story end at its end. Only the rain is real.

Facing the Wind

The Tsleil-Waututh nation's name in the Hunq'eme'nem language for Cates Park in North Vancouver is Whey-ah-Wichen, meaning "faces the wind"

Let them go into the wind, some part of me says,
and I do, I let them, the wind will take them
whatever I say or do, so I give them to the wind
to be refined to what they are and will be,
whatever I say or do. Then they run down the sand,
they turn and wave, I see they are waving goodbye,
their hair blowing horizontal across their faces,
the blue-green inlet waters rolling close
and almost breathing, they turn away again
to look out to fast-flying, white-winged waves,
they stay still, they wait for the tide to touch their shoes.
Then I am taken up where I stand, then I could step
over some brink in myself, except the wind
takes up every particle of cold grey sand
and every wave-crushed, wave-turned piece of shell
and every wave-smoothed piece of lost tree bark
while it takes me up, and takes up my small children
as the two of them truly are, have been, will be.
Let them go into the wind, some part of me says,
into the wind that plays like children who play
along a shore of seagulls, crows, scurrying crabs,
large rocks at rest for millennia, jellyfish, visiting seals—
plays in children's shouts, in their hands, their feet.
The wind utters wind, the waves recite waves—
the wind takes up the shore and us and gives no hint
it is aware it does this, and makes me want all the more
to plead and petition though I can expect no answer.

Paths

We have our thoroughfares, we have the descendants
of the wooden plank paths
laid down through the hacked and sawn and blasted forest—
now Lynn Valley Road, Mountain Highway.
We have our drives and avenues
cutting across where there were once fish-filled sloughs—
now Marine Drive, Bewicke Avenue.
But where are the paths
leading from river to river, from mountain lake to village,
from village to winter camp?
Where are they, the original paths of this place?
Like the routes within the rain-sounds,
like the routes the rain takes on winds
when the low heavens release it,
like the routes the sunlight takes through the rain—
they must still be here.
The new roads go from street to street,
machine to machine,
connect grid after grid.
The old roads must go
where the roads within people go—
the roads that vanish when a person dies,
yet while a person is alive
show the way through what does not stay to what stays.
Those paths that lead where they led
long, long before I was here,
they lead where I will be when I am gone and am nothing
except what I did not know of this place.

Kayak Music

The hands of each of them on the other
are the blade surfaces of the paddles

that they turn and pull through inlet water
with strokes for forward, reverse, sweep and spin.

The tide rolls in arriving at the full
and clasps the sand to the pull of the moon.

There is always the water lying down
remembering back to its beginning,

the fusion that is the sun. Rouse the child
waiting to open its eyes on the shore

of morning. The day will sleep. The water
is asking the paddles to propel the kayak.

There is nothing visible that is not
the invisible asking to be touched.

Blue

I

With a driftwood stick smoothed by the ocean waves,
you traced in the sand the first letters of an alphabet—
that was how you taught me a new word for water.
I thought I knew all the ways I would ever want
to say water—the waves arriving, the rivers and creeks
overflowing with rain coming down mountainsides
telling me where I had been born. But I sounded
out the word you spelled in your language
as if it were the first word I had ever learned.

If you have seen the river water draw long scarves
over the length of the changes in the riverbed
and the level run when the current slows to meet the inlet,
that is the way I let my hands learn the language of your skin.

If you have seen the ocean wind touch the leaves
of the sparse trees standing along a shore
where there was once only forest,
that is the way I let my hands outline what you have lost.

II

The shore before the shore, the shore before, before
and before, is not the shore that has ever appeared to me—
the colour I see when I look out at wave crests
is at once no colour and the bright white of bodiless bone.
The colour I see when I look up at the night sky
is at once no colour and the deep black of being thrown
into the darkness of my bones. At every instant
the ocean becomes a see-through wave that collapses,
and the ocean becomes a wave again.

On the shore of the afternoon, the sunlight's fire
burns at a cave entrance, and I see in the cave
a pair of silhouettes and wonder whether it is us.

With a driftwood stick smoothed by the ocean waves,
you traced in the sand a word for water—I learned it
as if unlearning my name, and saw the ocean and sky
were blue. As you traced the letters you told me
the word for blue in your language is the word for water.

If you have seen the sunlight fall into the stained
glass vaults of the stray flowers blooming wild
in the far-flinging grass along the sand, that is the way
I witness my own look enter your eyes. If you have seen
the deer come down from the mountains in the early morning,
moving past the leaves of the forest trees,
that is the way you brush against me.

III

The word in your language for blue is not the word
for blue—it is a word for not knowing, for what hides
from us, as when people had no way to describe blue
and it evaded sight, as when the sea was not blue
but *wine-dark*—the blue of not knowing
is the only blue of before and before and before.

With a driftwood stick smoothed by the ocean waves,
you showed me the word you knew for water.
You traced the letters the way waves arrive.
I learned the word for blue was "like water"
and could discern no colour that was not
like the colour of the water of where I had been born.

Still I wanted to say and discover blue.
If you have seen a glittering ocean wave bend,
that is the way you move and tell me without words
that you are here, nowhere except here; you arrive
and arrive. If you have seen the swerving creek water
form fists and split the knuckles of its need,
that is the way I have come to you.

If you have seen the ocean water marry light
by taking in all the wavelengths except blue,
which reflects and scatters, coming to the eye again,
that is the way you bring blue to me.
That is the way it is you who looks through me
when I say the word blue, and that is the way
there is always blue, even though there is no word for it
in your language except "like water."

IV

You found a driftwood stick smoothed by the ocean waves.
You were a teacher at a blackboard with a pointer
introducing first letters, indicating water, instructing me
in the first matter—having arrived here like the ocean waves
arrive and like the colour blue arrives and arrives—
and you taught me the word for water
so I could try to say what blue is like.

You found a driftwood stick smoothed by the ocean waves.
You traced in the sand the simplest word in your language
and brought blue to a shore like the ocean brings waves
to play and play. Though I know anyone who trusts only eyes
will only see their own and others' memorials,
and bury grey ash wherever they look, I know too
that when they love they let their names be no more
than the names of the water they look through,
and they themselves a mirror for every passing love.

Above the sand where I follow the sweeping curves
of your letters, it is blue, and with a driftwood stick
carried here by the ocean, you do away with the letters
as if erasing chalk, and the blue I imagine
leads me the way of blue before and before and before,
and leads me beyond the dimensions of a shore's canvas
of air and light, and beyond the name for blue
and therefore beyond names. If you have seen
how I move through water, fire, dust and air to find you,
and move through blue, that is the way
you will teach my hands, that is the way you will
root the tongue that knows the name of blue in my throat.

Drums

The lowest rent in town was on that block
across the street from where young men beat drums
all August from late evening until pre-dawn
and the sound came through my room in waves with the heat.
An hour after she arrived back, I threw
her travel case out the front door of the building.
Her clothes went scattering over the grass.
She had gone to a village in the north of BC
to deliver a program of free dental care.
In her letters, she complained about the mothers
who gave their kids bedtime baby bottles
filled with sugary juice that made their teeth rot.
She said I could take a small plane to visit her.
I never did. I was driving taxi
or in my place lying awake because of the drums.
Or standing by myself in clubs looking ridiculous
in hiking boots and creating harrowing hangovers.
The heat went on. The drums continued to beat.
I could hear little else. When she showed up again,
I could hear little of what she said to me,
even when she shouted in my face. When she left
and I decided I had to leave for Europe,
she insisted on driving me to the airport
to see me off. Even at the departure gate we fought.
The next day, in London on a layover,
drunk, I visited a fortune teller. He informed me
it was important that I leave a donation
of every type of coin at St. Martin-in-the-Fields
and fix my crooked front tooth. I never did.
When I got to Greece, she telephoned from Vancouver
to the school where I had a teaching position
to wish me all the best. *She must love you,*

the secretary said, who envisioned her fiancé
as a god. There was nothing I could say
that I would mean. In a city on the Greek plain,
I began and began to forget her. In the day,
there was light, and within the light, silence.
In the night, I heard drums. Violins, mandolins—drums.
In the building next door, bands played old songs
of the displaced Greeks of Asia Minor, the Greek
refugees of Greece. The drums continued. The beat
ran on beneath melodies that swerved and wailing
that told of the ones for whom home was not home.
The drums continued. I heard songs arise
from the beat and tell of the salmon returning
from the ocean to ascend creeks and spawn and die.
I heard chants arise and elicit the spirit in the form
of a woman running through a cedar forest swifter
than a doe to vanish in bright mist. I heard the steady,
low voices of men singing to be who they were.
The Greek drums continued. The Squamish drums
that belonged to where I had been born continued.
And the beating let arise from beneath my feet
what was as soon distant, and of the unknown place,
with its skin of the only drum of home.

Foal

When would she die? We knew it would be soon.
She had a few weeks. She had months, maybe.
Everything had happened so fast, and now—our mother—
when would she die?
Each time she tried
with the help of the walker to make it the five or six feet
from her bed to the bathroom and could not,
we knew the end was that much closer.
Each time she made it
to the dining room and could not sit in a chair
more than the couple of minutes
it took for her to try to eat a mouthful or two and give up,
then stood with our help
so that she could reach out and veer to the nearby couch.
Each time she fell,
each time she could not sit up in bed or could not breathe.
When would it be?
It was not that we wanted her to go.
We were holding on to her with everything we were.
It was that while we watched her,
week by week, day by day,
we saw death tricking her and us.
It was my mother
who had come to stay with us almost a year before
and now, as she changed literally overnight,
it was almost somebody else.
And now we went out for an hour
and when we returned,
my mother was nowhere to be seen
and there was a young foal in the apartment.
It was teetering taking its first steps
in the hallway between my mother's room

and the front room
and slipping on the hardwood.
A little more than thirty minutes later, it was bounding,
bewildered by the life in it,
and quickly enough, it was racing around and around
kicking up its hind legs against the walls.
Every unit of its energy was fuelling it
to do all it could to break out
of its sudden confinement,
every unit a precise one, an exact measure
of the life that had been stored in its wild, defiant body
from an indeterminate time
stretching back to when it did not yet exist,
and that it had to use now, now, now.

Finding the Character

In the care centre where she had sat up in bed,
my mother began calling out to people—
her parents, her sister, her children, her old friends ...
It went on for hours and hours. The oxygen
she was hooked up to seemed to literally inspire her.
The names kept coming, the conversations with the people
she called out to kept coming. *Paul?!* she cried out.
Paul?! Who was Paul? None of us knew.
Jack?! Who was he? None of us knew.
At one point, she returned to us.
Would you like to sleep, Mom?
No, she announced. *I want to talk.*

She paused briefly, and continued.
She was talking with so many people—
we realized we knew only a part of her.
I have to find the character! she said.
The talk was pouring out of her with such intensity,
we assumed it was delirium, autonomic response,
nonsense. Then it came back to me—
as a young woman, a single mother on welfare
with four kids, my mother had dreamt
of becoming an actress. She had had no chance
to do anything about it decades ago, but now,
staring straight ahead, she was calling out
the names of characters from *The Young and the Restless*,
and saying lines as if she were reading from a teleprompter.
While she had breath left, my mother was imagining
she had landed a role in a famous daytime soap.

Old, diseased, tired beyond tired (but not in pain,
not in pain!), she was suddenly filled with energy
in the middle of a fabulous life—great, episodic,
passionate affairs, devastating betrayals,
ecstatic reunions, new hairstyles every week,
new outfits, familial treachery, devotions of the heart
lasting season after season, bouts of madness,
aftermaths of serene wisdom, seduction,
humiliation, candlelit dinners—she was falling
and she was being redeemed over and over,
returning to impossible joy. For eighteen hours straight,
talking non-stop, she was alive in the melodrama
of the small screen, her life an incredible script—
and her life her audience. She talked as an actress
doing an extended end-of-series monologue,
until she fell asleep, never to wake again,
just as she found her character, young and restless.

My Mother and Elvis

My mother loved Sam Elliott and Kevin Costner
and more recently, Idris Elba—but more than any
of these men she loved Elvis. She loved Elvis.
Elvis was her king. "Love Me Tender," "Hound Dog,"
"Blue Suede Shoes," "Return to Sender,"
"In the Ghetto"—his songs were her holy music.
She beheld him in the flesh once in Las Vegas.
After that she knew the man with the lip and hips,
sideburns and voice meant only for her,
handsomer than a hundred movie stars,
a miracle of sexuality, would live forever.
She was Elvis-crazy to the end. When Elvis died
bloated and sad, my mother worshipped him more.
When she had shrunk, eighty, cancer-ridden,
could breathe only with an oxygen machine,
we brought her a White Spot mushroom burger,
fries and chocolate shake. She ate and drank,
a little anyway, smiled like a cute teen
and announced: "Heaven." It was Elvis,
Elvis, Elvis ... and she fell back
in the hospital bed as if she might faint
like a frantic fan of nothing but air.

Then the Rain Came

It spirited itself here so quickly
that it could not be called rain. The cold drops
splattering against the glass were the hands
of person after person arriving
with no memory of where they came from
and no knowledge of where they were going
yet desperate to find a way through
and to stay. My mother, who loved seeing
and hearing wild rain, sat up abruptly
in the institutional bed, face pressed
to a window invisible to me,
staring out like a wide-eyed, wizened child.
"I'm not ready," she said. "This doesn't feel right."

The quiet that came at another hour
was sudden rain that had ended as soon
as it started and seemed to be waiting
to come back, start again—but she was gone.

Icon

In half-hidden holy places
I have found myself entering,
rough stone hovels of the spirit,
icons have always been waiting.
And though they are painted on wood—
white, red, blue—they are not relics
or miracle iconography;
no one proclaims they show the work
of more than simple human hands.
Still, they hang serene on white walls,
sit on shelves in faithful alcoves,
illuminated with fine jars
of olive oil burning on wicks—
still they keep the deepest secrets,
still they are the clearest windows.

The days after my mother died,
I looked repeatedly at what
I knew of her and saw images
from stories people had told me
about a sparkling, wild young girl
and from my memories of her—
griefs, humiliations, triumphs,
failed marriages, successful ones—
all begin to gather themselves
together in a single place,
the disparate times of her life
meeting and making perfect sense.
Natural sight, familiar belief—
they surrender their hold on me,
and no lines of my mother's life
converge in the unseen distance
or move towards nothingness;
those vanishing points are outside
of this place, in front of its frame.
As far away as she has seemed,
I see she is close. I look at her
and, simple and vast, she looks back.

At the service we held for her
in a small modest old chapel,
as my brothers and I recalled
my mother, none of us aware
of details recalled by the others,
yet each of us full of those details,
it was as if we were at work
filling in the distinct outlines
in partially abstract pictures.
No saint, yet a saint, my mother
was being purified in us;
our recollections of her arose
within us to display someone
who was wholly her and not her.

It is as if everything is finished now,
everything has touched a beginning,
a source, and my mother has been
transformed into a primitive icon:
two-dimensional, costumed
in the complete, unmixed colours
of the human and the divine,
unrecognizable to us except
in the delicate, endless green
of the eyes through which she sees.

The Fine Print

No one reads the fine print.
You sign your name, you initial,
you check a box and click submit
below a pageful of text.
You acknowledge, you agree.

Later, you are referred back to it.
The benefits you thought would be automatic—
the fine print dictates otherwise.
You're too old. No, you're too young.
Your medical history has been flagged.
You didn't mention a criminal record.

Yes, you made monthly payments year after year—
but the fine print was always there,
and the conditions attached to your claim—
lettering so small and concentrated that it
runs together and becomes a slow black river—
were always determining your little fate.

Whoever writes the fine print must write it
for you on the day you are born,
and mean it to hold until your memorial service—
the eulogy, the prayers, the songs,
the large photo of you
will say you were this and this
and what is about to happen
to you is this and this.

No one reads the fine print.
And the river of lettering wouldn't stop if you did—
the qualifying, the disqualifying, etcetera.
You acknowledge, you agree ...
It's only below the surface current
that you can move in accord
with a different current—always starting again—
no fine print to read or not read.
Here you owe nothing, you want nothing,
in the black flowing of the undertow.

Beggar

Rain arrives like a beggar at the door.
You hear the wind and the quick knocking, go lift the latch,
and there he is, a chaos of radiant mist and flying drops
concentrated into a leaning figure, eyes colourless,
speech uttered as at a distance, the words unknown to you
but relaying clearly to you that he is asking you
for whatever you can give. What can you give?

You do not know how, but you give him your memories,
the ones that occur to you this instant—
you give him the sound, smell, sight, taste, touch.
He pockets them deftly, taking them the way
he would a handful of coins, knowing immediately
the exact total value, measuring with the dimensions
of his pockets the mirroring silver of what you want.
He shivers, the cold increasing through his cells,
but he does not want to come in, houses are not for him.
He wants to say hello, you understand this.
And he wants to say goodbye, as he is here
and he is elsewhere where there are no hellos
or goodbyes. The drops that constitute him
are footholds he has used to make his way to your door,
the path disappearing forever behind him.
When he falls in front of you, he gathers himself up
and asks you again for whatever you can give.

You give him what you can, you give him more
of your memories, while the rain rings its pure tone
like a tuning fork scattering through the air.
You give him what you can and he counts it,
he measures it. His pockets fill while your pockets
empty. His pockets are bottomless, and you see
that the units of exchange he uses are beyond you.
You discover any memory you give resonates
at perfect pitch at the touch of what you want.
While he continues to speak to you, his words
are less words than vibrations in your ears,
and they inform you of where they begin travelling
farther than you can hear. While he fills and fills
his pockets, you continue to give and give until
finally it is clear that all you will ever remember
is what you want, and all you will ever want
is to give what you are to the rain as if offering alms.

While You Brushed Your Hair

While you brushed your hair,
while you brushed your hair down
to the small of your back and then for a moment
carried the flow of your hair within the half-circle
of your held-out thumb and fingers—
while you brushed your hair,
the river called Chay-Chul-Wuk
flowed and straightened through
the spaces between rocks.

The river water swerved and swept out
and hurried through a narrow channel
and swept out and swirled in eddies
and turned through mazes of rocks
and straightened again before the start
of its calm run to the inlet.
While you brushed your hair,
the river flowed, while you flicked
and swayed the length and weight
of your hair in front of a mirror
in which I could see myself
at the back of the room, watching you.

While you brushed your hair,
while I witnessed it flow and straighten,
and straighten and flow, it flowed as the river
flowed through its name, through a meaning
I did not know. But I said the name of the river
over and over while you brushed your hair
down to the small of your back
and the river called Chay-Chul-Wuk
flowed and straightened through the spaces
between rocks on its way to the inlet—
while you brushed your hair.

Brass Ring

You go out for a celebratory dinner together
and a waiter directs the two of you
through the candlelit restaurant to your table
like an attendant taking children around a carousel
to lift them onto the painted wooden horses.
You toast each other, reminisce, commemorate
the circle you have gone around again;
an arriving tear counts every other tear,
a joy spins into another joy, the hands of a clock
show the hour of a first date, a first touch, a kiss.
And this while a set of recorded songs repeats
like looped circus music, and the children you are
hold on while your horses gallop into a dark,
then reappear in mirrored and gilded electric light
to step onto a circular platform again—
your anniversary returns you here. You ride and ride,
you want the flashing ring; you try your luck—
if you reach and snatch it from its rail,
you know you must throw it into the dark.
Your horses will vanish and reappear without riders,
and your anniversary is for you to remember
as far back as you can to when you do not know
whom it is you love, or who it is who loves.

Greek Fire

There is an old story, old and hidden,
and we cannot know its origin, yet we witness it set a moment ablaze,
as when someone has hidden a thing with infinite care

then forgotten where they hid it, and then others discover it.
History says there was once an incendiary weapon—
a fire that ignited on contact with water and burned on water

and could not be extinguished with water. The formula for the weapon
was a guarded secret, and was lost, and remains unknown.
And so history explains it—water is a bridge

for a fire to come into the world. And this was the way it was
with the two us—we were fire walking on water
and burning all the more brightly because we burned on water.

History says the brass head of a lion
was mounted at the prow of a ship—a siphon pump and a swivelling
    nozzle
shot the mixture out through the lion's mouth

launching streams of flames that leapt into radiance
filling the sea waves and incinerating everything in their path.
For our part, we were bewildered,

we were ships meeting in battle, and we shared a kind of hate,
and each overthrew the other in the to-fro spectacle.
And there is the old story, dateless, and in it

the love that cannot go to all, because it is of the body,
must be the enemy. And this too was the way it was with us—
except the all I wanted to go to was all of you,

and if the burning water of a story
is love freed from time, then we were two enemies
allowed to kiss forever within a moment, and the formula lost.

Great with Tigers

... great with tigers ...
    —William Shakespeare, *Timon of Athens*

The smell of menstruation moves through the apartment—
I imagine filaments stretching and folding in patterns.

The first tampon is in the bathroom wastebasket;
I take a shower and the fumes float up within the caressing steam.

She is in the front room going through dance routines—
she will be menstruating while she teaches her classes, dancing in her
    blood flow.

I hear her counting beats. Her counting ends, it begins again—
the heart of a lithe one in high grass undergoing the seconds.

The ovum is breaking up, and the power in it that can produce a person
is vibrating through the apartment; I hear her again in her final hour of
    labour.

I drive the children to school—the moon inordinately bright, and the wet
    sun rising.
The first morning bell rings; the doors swing out for the throng.

I go back for them in the afternoon—the two of them run shouting
into the charged air and take my hands and lead me.

When, within the gateway of her womb, she could feel the unborn
kicking and rolling, she sang to them and made them dance in the animal
    light;

they danced, they were brightening wine in her womb's glass, they were
  calm.
Now her womb sheds its inner layer, and the scent she conceived comes
  through.

Three nights in a row, I have dreamt of tigers,
and sensed their arrival, and felt them as they advanced silently,

with great fluidity through the front room, the bedroom—
the scent magnetic and deeper than that of blood or earth;

the scent of a vintage not of any year but of moments beyond number.
Now while her womb is full not of the child said to know all things

but of what is invisible, the whole apartment is a womb, the abode of a
  fragrance;
the tiger of what I cannot know goes stalking through space.

My Mother's Last Birthday Dinner

I

None of us knows that this will be her last birthday dinner. We see only that she is different, more herself than usual. She eats with us and laughs and seems young. She remembers dozens of western films, and all the main actors. She knows every player on the Canucks. Every Elvis song. Every member of every family and the addresses on the streets where she has lived. Every old flame of each of her sons. Her memories that belong more deeply to her—though they can never be shared with us, we see them shining in her; they tell me that the senses at their height are every kind of love. And time is only a way to remember.

II

We sit around her at a modest but beautiful table. My mother is already becoming a spirit. We are astonished at how quickly she eats, and how much. Almost as soon as they are served to her from the communal restaurant plate, the roasted potatoes vanish. The food she prefers above all other foods—it is as if it, too, is transforming into spirit. As her time runs out, the starch of the potatoes is running out, and since she is still here, becoming lighter and lighter, she must eat and eat.

III

Then, in the middle of the dinner, memories that are my mother's pass into me. They become a part of my memories of her and are like invisible layers of light. The memories will stay in me—but will be gone when I am gone; she communicates this to me silently, even as she makes small talk. She smiles at me. She is more alive now than she has ever been. She seems to know it. All through her birthday dinner, she has been preparing to step into an elsewhere.

IV

While she is still able as a living person, my mother smiles at me, and smiles in turn at the three other aging men sitting around her. Then, in the candlelight of the restaurant we see the face of the spirit that is my mother. It is the face that appeared to us before our recollections of anyone arose within us, and before we remembered anyone's name. And then the spirit circles around us like a single breath, and each of the four of us sees my mother smiling into his eyes in the moments just after he was born.

When the Whales Return

They are reporting that orcas have been sighted
swimming into the inlet for the first time in eighty years—
a mother and her four young, the baby fins visible
alongside the mother's, the five of them rolling and jumping
and spuming and puffing after the big breaths,
breaching in and out of the deep, dark-blue waters,
following the whale ways of quietness opening now
as a pandemic halts ship traffic up and down the coast.
A week ago, my mother went her own way alone into the silence
and is all around me but beyond anyone's call,
where her spirit's sonar must be sending out signals
that bounce back to her to tell her where she is going
but from beyond what I know as hearing or distance.
The orcas on their long, echoing ocean paths
bring with them the silences they pass through,
they come now into the harbour and along the shoreline
at the bottom of the avenue where my mother would walk
with me in her womb, a girl carrying a tiny new heartbeat
that had joined her own in the space she discovered in her,
the way cleared for her because of her twirling joy.
Like the orcas that have never swum here before
but have found their way, she found her way in her life
through the mysterious silence she knew was love.
Those moments when love arrived and moved within her,
and took her up in its ceaseless play and led her,
were the moments when she was most herself
through her eighty years. Now that she is gone,
and the world is locked down, it must still be leading her.
It was right that she died as the city streets began
to go quiet and the ocean began to go quiet.
There was always a quietness within my spinning,
laughing mother when she was happiest—

almost hypnotizing her, making her say that she wished
everything would stop, stay exactly as it was forever,
as it stops now and allows great silences to arise and travel
from the ocean into the inlet under bridges, past skyscrapers,
and roll alongside the shoreline when the whales return.

Glass

My mother's mother worked her entire adult life
as a secretary for a large glass-manufacturing company.
In her adolescence, her teachers had told her
that she should continue her education, become a teacher—
the advice of the era for a girl two grades ahead in school.
But she chose instead to graduate and go straight into a job
and marry a man with a thicket of red hair and sparkling blue eyes.
And whenever a family member or friend needed glass—
a new panel for a door, a new pane for a picture window—
she would perform her magic at work and get that person a deal.

And late at night, with pen and paper, with typewriter,
sometimes right through to morning, she would write out
not product orders or price lists, but plots and images of love
in story after story, in poem after poem;
she would type out not invoices or bosses' letters,
but the syllables for the music she heard in her head;
and copy down not minutes of meetings, but movements
of lit sea waves that lifted, arced and broke through her—
emblems all around her of the red-haired man and herself
on a shore of wild driftwood and many-faceted sand grains.

Nights now at my computer, where I am the secretary
on the job of my life, when I need the right word
I consult a dictionary she bought me for my school supplies.
When I see assemblages of words—subtle signs,
interlacing rays issuing out of the common dark—
I feel she is there, I believe she is advising me to see past
my eyes' instructions to the beginnings of all eyes,
and then I address the sacred air and I address her;
she makes her way to me bringing me the things of the world
to look through, and it is as if I look through glass.

Last Rites

She would live a long life, though not long enough
to see me middle-aged and see my children.
She would live a long life—though no one thought
she would when in 1918, in a town at the edge of Boston
where she was born and where her parents stayed
ten years on their way from the old country
to the west coast of Canada, she lay in her bed delirious,
a seven-year-old girl sick with the Spanish Flu.
The doctor said she would be dead by morning.
A religious official going up and down the street
providing last rites was brought in to give her a blessing.

And then in the morning she woke and sat up
clear-eyed, fever and weakness gone—perfectly well again.
She would live a long life, and the following spring,
when her parents finally arrived with her and her younger sister
at the sandy shore where her father built a makeshift home,
she entered the first months of her ninth year
among the driftwood and near the sea waves and seagulls,
and she ran where the rays of the sun led her all summer.

It is the same shore where I now bring my two children—
around the age she was when she was brought here.
I watch while the light that turns here introduces itself
to them the way it did to her a hundred years ago.
It anoints them, it performs a laying-on of hands
as its rays reach their eyes and give themselves away
and gather themselves up again in air and wave crests
and in the same sand my grandmother stepped onto
and looked out from in the year after her miracle recovery.
She would live a long life, and grow old visiting this shore
where my children now play alone in the sun
while a new pandemic begins to spread. She would live,
and the only last rites ever true for her would be rites
repeated when sea waves arrive or when new births
take light from one person to another and another.

Nests

A large woven cup left for light to fill—
filtering away twig by twig, strand by strand;
the skeleton where the blind days arrive
and reach with my hands, my earth out of earth.
My keychain chimes; my front door locks, unlocks.
Birds pass into birds. I carry a cry
of abandonment; I cannot hear it.
Light is turning everywhere, forever.
Love and care, I know, make a house a charm
against our vanishing. While time opens
curtains in us. Windows defeat windows.

Fledglings are pushed, and they fall, nudged and buoyed
when they plummet trying to work wings right.
Light digging graves in leaves. There is a bird
to take words where only birds go; it flings
itself into the air. Those who call, call
and concentrate the day and wear one face.
That face breaks into many. Light that meets
my face is made of the dead. The moment
of love releases the moment; the eyes
must cast their judgment and must undo it.
What I see goes free, comes back, rebuilds nests.

Notes & Acknowledgements

The title of this collection is taken from a line in the D.H. Lawrence poem, "Flowers and Men" ("Oh what in you can answer to this blueness?").

"Greek Fire"—Greek Fire (also called "sea fire") was a liquid concoction heated, pressurized, then delivered via siphon. It was used by the Byzantine Greeks during battles at sea. The "old story" here is an imagined neo-Platonic love story of love stories.

Many thanks to the editors of the publications in which some of the poems in this book first appeared:

The Antigonish Review—"Story of Mist"
Canadian Literature—"Paths"
Cascadia—"Shore"; "Facing the Wind"
The Dalhousie Review—"Greek Fire"
FreeFall—"The Fine Print"; "While You Brushed Your Hair"
Juniper—"A Cup of Coffee"
Literary Review of Canada—"When the Whales Return"
long con magazine—"The Blue Boy"
Maple Tree Literary Supplement—"Debt"; "Kayak Music"; "Glass"
Vallum—"Exit"
The Walrus—"Dumpster"

Gratitude to Silas White for his editing of this collection. Immense thanks to Nicola Goshulak for her notes. And thanks to everyone at Harbour Publishing.

About the Author

Russell Thornton's *The Hundred Lives* (Quattro Books, 2014) was short-listed for the Griffin Poetry Prize. His *Birds, Metals, Stones & Rain* (Harbour Publishing, 2013) was shortlisted for the Governor General's Literary Award for Poetry, the Raymond Souster Award and the Dorothy Livesay Poetry Prize. His other titles include *The Fifth Window* (Thistledown Press, 2000), *A Tunisian Notebook* (Seraphim Editions, 2002), *House Built of Rain* (Harbour Publishing, 2003; shortlisted for the Dorothy Livesay Poetry Prize and the ReLit Award for poetry), *The Human Shore* and *The Broken Face* (Harbour Publishing, 2006 and 2018). Thornton's poetry has appeared in several anthologies and as part of BC's Poetry in Transit. He lives in North Vancouver, BC.